Tools for Problem Solving

Level C

STECK-VAUGHN ®
C O M P A N Y

A Division of Harcourt Brace & Company

Acknowledgments

Executive Editor	**Diane Sharpe**
Senior Project Editor	**Donna Rodgers**
Editor	**Allison Welch**
Design Project Manager	**Sheryl Cota**
Cover Design	**John Harrison**
Electronic Production	**PC&F, Inc.**
Photography	**Cover:** © Joe Viesti/The Viesti Collection; p. 1 © Joe Viesti/The Viesti Collection; p. 4 © Mark Wagner/ Tony Stone Images; pp. 5, 7 © Rusty Kaim; p. 8 © Alese/ MortPECHTER/The Stock Market; p. 9 © Rusty Kaim; p. 11 © Jan Kopec/Tony Stone Images; p. 12 © Superstock; p. 16 © Gordon R. Gainer/The Stock Market; p. 17 © Frank Rossotto/ The Stock Market; p. 18 © Superstock; p. 19 © Michael Habicht/ Earth Scenes; p. 22 © Park Street; p. 25 © PhotoDisc; p. 49 © Superstock; p. 50 (t) © Tony Freeman/PhotoEdit; p. 50 (m, b) © Superstock; p. 56 © Jose Carrillo/PhotoEdit; p. 57 (m) © Tony Freeman/PhotoEdit; p. 58 © Tony Freeman/PhotoEdit; p. 60 (t) © Mark Gamba/The Stock Market; p. 66 (m) © Warren Lynch & Associates/FoodPix; p. 74 © Superstock; p. 76 © PhotoDisc; Additional photography by Digital Studios.
Illustration	pp. 10, 13, 15, 21, 31–37, 40, 43, 45, 46, 56–58, 70–72, 78, 80 Dave Blanchette.

ISBN 0-8172-8127-4

Copyright © 1999 Steck-Vaughn Company

Contents

Up, Up, and Away!

Lesson 1   Write a Plan

Suppose you were the pilot of a hot air balloon. One weekend, you flew 56 miles. The next weekend, you flew 25 miles. How many miles did you fly in all?

Write a plan to solve the problem.

Step 1
Write in your own words what you need to find out.

_____

_____

Step 2
Write the facts that will be useful.

_____

_____

Step 3
Explain or show how you will solve the problem.

_____

_____

_____

_____

Writing a Plan: Addition and Subtraction

Make a Model

Try using base ten blocks to solve the problem.

> **R**ead the problem again. Use base ten blocks to show the number of miles you flew.

Remember:
56 = 5 tens 6 ones
25 = 2 tens 5 ones

1. Model the number of miles flown the first weekend, 56 miles. Use tens strips and ones cubes.

   _____ tens _____ ones

2. Model the number of miles flown the next weekend, 25 miles. Use tens strips and ones cubes.

   _____ tens _____ ones

3. Add the ones. Regroup to state them as tens and ones.

   _____ ones = _____ tens _____ ones

4. Then add the tens. Include what you had to regroup.   _____ tens

5. How many miles in all did you fly on these weekends?   _____ miles

6. How much farther did the balloon fly on the first weekend than on the next one? Use the blocks to subtract.   _____ miles

Practice

Here are three problems for you.

Quick-Solve 1

Suppose a balloon leaves Dallas with 54 pounds of cargo. In Oklahoma City, 28 more pounds are added. How much cargo does the balloon have in all?

Quick-Solve 2

One balloon traveled 39 miles on Friday. Then it flew 41 miles on Saturday. How many miles did it travel in both days?

Quick-Solve 3

At a balloon rally in Atlanta, 26 balloons finished the race. A total of 77 balloons were entered. How many balloons did not finish the race?

Use What You Know

One balloon flew 28 miles on Friday. Then it flew 19 miles on Saturday. How much farther did the balloon fly on Friday than on Saturday?

> **Remember:**
> 1 ten = 10 ones

Use base ten blocks to show the distance the balloon flew on Friday. Subtract blocks to show the distance flown on Saturday. Look at the blocks that are left. What is the difference?

1. Model the number of miles flown on Friday, 28 miles. Use tens strips and ones cubes.

   _____ tens _____ ones

2. The balloon flew 19 miles on Saturday. Can you subtract 9 ones from 8 ones? _____

3. Regroup 28 so you will have enough ones to subtract. Then you will have fewer tens and more ones.

   2 tens 8 ones = _____ tens _____ ones

4. Now you can subtract the ones. Then subtract the tens.

   _____ tens _____ ones

5. How much farther did the balloon fly on Friday than on Saturday? _____ miles

6. What if you add the distance flown on these two days? How far did the balloon fly in all? _____ miles

Making a Model: Addition and Subtraction

Lesson 2 Write a Plan

One weekend, there was a hot air balloon rally near Dallas. One balloon landed 115 feet from the target. Another balloon landed 133 feet from the target. How much closer to the target did the first balloon land?

Write a plan to solve the problem.

Step 1   Write in your own words what you need to find out.

_____

_____

Step 2   Write the facts that will be useful.

_____

_____

Step 3   Explain or show how you will solve the problem.

_____

_____

_____

_____

_____

Make a Model

Try using base ten blocks to solve the problem.

Regroup when you don't have enough ones to subtract.

> **U**se the blocks to show the farther distance from the target. Then subtract the distance of the closer balloon. How much closer to the target did it land?

1. Model the number of feet from the target of the farther balloon, 133 feet. Use hundreds flats, tens strips, and ones cubes.

   _____ hundreds _____ tens _____ ones

2. The closer balloon landed 115 feet from the target.

   Can you subtract 5 ones from 3 ones? _____

3. Regroup to get more ones. Then rename 133 with fewer tens and more ones.

   _____ hundreds _____ tens _____ ones

4. Now you can subtract the ones. Then subtract the tens and hundreds.

   _____ hundreds _____ tens _____ ones

5. How much closer to the target did the first balloon land? _____ feet

6. One of the first balloons was 72 feet around. A modern balloon can be about 120 feet around.

   What is the difference in these sizes? _____ feet

Practice

Here are three problems for you.

Quick-Solve 1

One balloon flew 357 miles in a year. Another balloon flew 223 miles in a year. How much farther did the first balloon fly?

Quick-Solve 2

The prize money for first place at one rally was $350. The prize for second place was $275. How much more was the prize money for first place?

Quick-Solve 3

The pilot of a balloon wants to carry 250 pounds of cargo. Which items can he take?

Cargo List	
telescopes	145 pounds
nylon rope	100 pounds
radios	75 pounds
parachutes	25 pounds

Use What You Know

One year, there were about 650 balloons at the Albuquerque Balloon Festival. Four years later, there were about 800 balloons there. About how many more balloons were there that year?

Remember:
1 hundred = 10 tens

Use the blocks to show the greater number of balloons. Then subtract the number of balloons in the first year. Regroup if you need to.

1. Model the greater number of balloons at the festival. Use hundreds flats, tens strips, and ones cubes.

   _____ hundreds _____ tens _____ ones

2. Try to subtract 650. Can you subtract the ones? _____

   Can you subtract the tens? _____

3. Regroup to get more tens. Then rename 800 with fewer hundreds and more tens.

   _____ hundreds _____ tens _____ ones

4. Subtract. How many hundreds, tens, and ones are left?

   _____ hundreds _____ tens _____ ones

5. How many more balloons were there four years after the first year? _____ balloons

Lesson 3   Make an Estimate

You have made a model with base ten blocks to solve problems. Now try making an estimate to solve a problem.

You can make an estimate by rounding a number to the nearest ten.

A balloon rally in Kansas lasted three days. The total distances that four of the balloons flew are listed in the table. About how many miles did they fly combined?

1. Round each number to the nearest 10. Then add.

Balloon	Actual Miles	Rounded Miles
Hot Shot	43	
Snake	58	
Cloud Man	71	
Zinger	92	

= about _____ miles

2. The total distance all four of the balloons traveled was

_____ (greater, less) than 200 miles.

3. Which two balloons flew about 100 miles combined? Explain how you found out.

_____

_____

_____

Making an Estimate: Addition and Subtraction

Practice

Here are three practice problems for you.

Quick-Solve 1

You want to buy souvenirs at a rally. You have $20. Which two souvenirs can you buy?

Souvenir	Cost
mini-balloon	$12
balloon mobile	$16
balloon book	$4
pinwheel	$3

Quick-Solve 2

If one balloon is 56 feet in diameter and another balloon has a diameter of 47 feet, about how much larger in diameter is the first balloon?

Quick-Solve 3

Anna received prize money in the amounts of $137, $150, and $75 from three balloon rallies. About how much money did she receive for the three rallies?

Use What You Know

You learned how to make an estimate with addition.
Now try making an estimate with subtraction.

If you need help, look back to page 12.

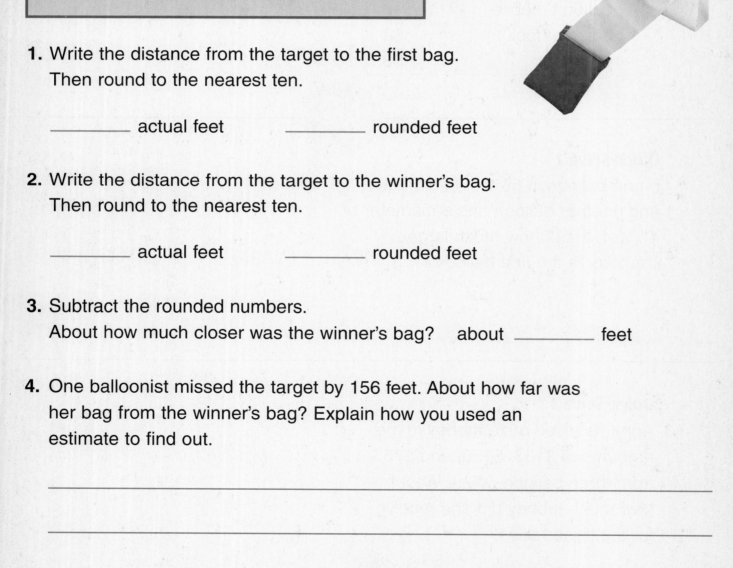

Sometimes a balloon rally is based on dropping a birdseed bag closest to the target. One balloonist dropped his bag 32 feet from the target. The winner dropped her bag only 14 feet from the target. About how much closer was her bag?

1. Write the distance from the target to the first bag. Then round to the nearest ten.

   _____ actual feet   _____ rounded feet

2. Write the distance from the target to the winner's bag. Then round to the nearest ten.

   _____ actual feet   _____ rounded feet

3. Subtract the rounded numbers. About how much closer was the winner's bag?   about _____ feet

4. One balloonist missed the target by 156 feet. About how far was her bag from the winner's bag? Explain how you used an estimate to find out.

   _____

   _____

   _____

Lesson 4   Solve It Your Way

Read each problem and decide how you will find the solution.

You may want to choose one of these strategies for each problem.

Make a Model
Make an Estimate

1. One balloon weighs 76 pounds. Another balloon weighs 92 pounds. How much do the two balloons weigh together?

2. A stand selling hot dogs at a rally made $334 one weekend. A stand selling colas made $523. About how much did they make combined?

3. Some National Championships have about 200 balloon entries. One year, there were 312 entries. About how many more balloons entered that year? Round to the nearest ten.

4. Tom drove the chase truck while his wife flew their balloon. He drove 60 miles of winding dirt roads to follow her. She flew 35 miles in a straight line. How many more miles did Tom drive than his wife flew?

5. An ad for one gas balloon company said that they could carry 600 pounds. A man called to ask if they could carry 550 pounds of sand and let him go along for the ride. What was their answer? Why?

6. A team from New Mexico has won 23 trophies this year. A team from Texas has won 34 trophies. If they both entered 50 races, which team lost about as often as it won?

Practice

Now write your own problems using addition and subtraction.

Quick-Solve 1

The answer to the problem is "43 pounds."
Write your own problem and share it with a
friend. If your friend does not get the same
answer, discuss how you might change the
problem or the solution to match.

Quick-Solve 2

The answer to the problem is "More than 100."
Write your own problem and share it with a friend.
If your friend does not get the same answer,
discuss how you might change the problem or the
solution to match.

Quick-Solve 3

The answer to the problem is "About 450 miles."
Write your own problem to share with a friend.
If your friend does not get the same answer,
discuss how you might change the problem or
the solution to match.

Review   Show What You Know

Work in a small group. Suppose a balloonist invites
you to go for a ride. He tells you that he can allow a
total of 300 pounds for you and your guests. Estimate
the number of friends you can invite to ride with you.

1. If you and your friends each weigh about 60 pounds,
   could 6 of you go on this balloon ride?
   How do you know?

   _____

   _____

2. Suppose you ask an adult to be one of your guests. If the adult
   weighs 150 pounds and you weigh 60 pounds, how many more
   friends could you invite?

   _____

3. If you and your friends weigh about 70 pounds each, how does
   that change the number you can invite?

   _____

   _____

4. Most balloon makers design a model of their balloon before
   making the real balloon. Design your own balloon.
   Draw it below or make a model.

UNIT 2   Shape Up!

The distance around a rectangle is called its *perimeter*.

Lesson 1   Write a Plan

Mrs. Riley's class is helping in a "Shape Up Our School" program. One group is designing a flower garden. It will be a rectangle that is 6 feet long and 3 feet wide. What will the distance around the garden be?

Write a plan to solve the problem.

Step 1

Write in your own words what you need to find out.

_____

_____

Step 2

Write the facts that will be useful.

_____

_____

Step 3

Explain or show how you will solve the problem.

_____

_____

_____

_____

Writing a Plan: Perimeter

Draw a Picture

Try making a drawing to show the garden.

Remember that opposite sides of a rectangle have the same length.

Draw a rectangle that is 6 units long and 3 units wide.
Let the distance between each dot represent one foot.
What is the distance around the garden?

1. Draw a rectangle that is 6 units long and 3 units wide.

   . . . .

   . . . .

   . . . .

   . . . .

   . . . .

2. Add the two longer sides.

   _____ + _____ = _____ units

3. Add the two shorter sides.

   _____ + _____ = _____ units

4. Add the sums of the longer and shorter sides.

   _____ + _____ = _____ units

5. What is the distance around the garden? _____ feet

6. Can you get the same answer by counting all the units around your drawing? How do you know?

   _____

   _____

Practice

Here are three practice problems for you.

Quick-Solve 1

Find the distance around this rectangle.
Each unit represents one foot.

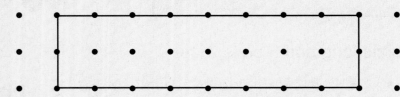

Quick-Solve 2

Find the distance around this square.
Each unit represents one foot.

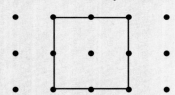

Quick-Solve 3

Find the perimeter of this rectangle.
Each unit represents one foot.

Use What You Know

One group of students wants to decorate a bulletin board for the "Shape Up Our School" program. The width of the board is 4 feet and its length is 5 feet. How many feet of border will they need for the edge of the bulletin board?

If you need help, look back to pages 18 and 19.

Draw a rectangle to represent the bulletin board. Then count or add the sides. How many feet of border will be needed?

1. Draw a rectangle that is 4 units wide and 5 units long.

```
•   •   •   •   •   •   •   •   •

•   •   •   •   •   •   •   •   •

•   •   •   •   •   •   •   •   •

•   •   •   •   •   •   •   •   •

•   •   •   •   •   •   •   •   •
```

2. Add all four sides.

_____ + _____ + _____ + _____ = _____ units

3. What is the perimeter of the board? _____ feet

4. How many feet of border will be needed? _____ feet

5. How could you find the distance around the board without adding all the sides?

Lesson 2 Write a Plan

Another group of students is putting mulch in a garden. If the length of the garden is 5 feet and the width is 3 feet, what is the area they will cover?

Area is the amount of room inside a figure.

Write a plan to solve the problem.

Step 1 Write in your own words what you need to find out.

_____

_____

Step 2 Write the facts that will be useful.

_____

_____

Step 3 Explain or show how you will solve the problem.

_____

_____

_____

_____

_____

_____

Draw a Picture

Try drawing a picture to solve the area problem.

> Draw a rectangle to represent the garden. Let the distance between each dot represent one foot. What is the area of the garden?

 You can check your answer by using centimeter cubes inside the rectangle.

1. Draw a rectangle that is 5 units long and 3 units wide.

2. Draw lines between the inside dots to fill the rectangle with squares.

3. How many squares are inside the rectangle? _____ squares

4. What is the area of the garden? _____ square feet

5. Look at your drawing. Area is always measured by a number of square units. Why do you think this is so?

_____

_____

6. Explain how you might use centimeter cubes to check the area of your drawing.

_____

_____

Practice

Here are three practice problems for you.
Draw a picture or use centimeter cubes to solve.

Quick-Solve 1

The top of Mr. Wu's desk is 2 feet wide and 4 feet long. What is the area of the desk top?

. . . . .

. . . . .

. . . . .

. . . . .

Quick-Solve 2

What is the area of a square block of grass that has sides of 4 feet?

. . . . .

. . . . .

. . . . .

. . . . .

. . . . .

Quick-Solve 3

Shade the rectangle that has the greater area.

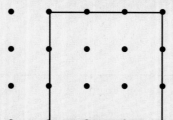

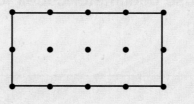

Applying Strategies

Use What You Know

Melissa and Alan are helping clean out two plant beds around the school. Melissa's plant bed is 9 feet long and 3 feet wide. Alan's plant bed is 7 feet long and 4 feet wide. Who has more area to clean out?

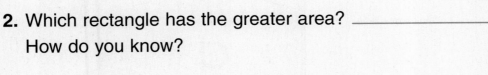

If you need help, look back to pages 22 and 23.

1. Draw each rectangle on the dot paper below.

· · · · · · · · · · · ·

· · · · · · · · · · · ·

· · · · · · · · · · · ·

· · · · · · · · · · · ·

· · · · · · · · · · · ·

· · · · · · · · · · · ·

· · · · · · · · · · · ·

· · · · · · · · · · · ·

· · · · · · · · · · · ·

· · · · · · · · · · · ·

2. Which rectangle has the greater area? _____
How do you know?

_____

_____

_____

3. Does Melissa or Alan have more area to clean out? _____

Lesson 3   Guess and Check

You have drawn pictures to solve problems.
Now try guessing and checking to solve problems.

Remember that *perimeter* is the distance around a shape.

Four groups of students made stickers for "Shape Up Our School" week. Guess the perimeter of each sticker below. Then check by using a centimeter ruler or centimeter cubes.

1.

Guess. _____ centimeters

Check. _____ centimeters

2.

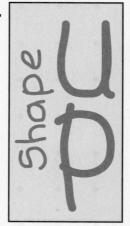

Guess. _____ centimeters

Check. _____ centimeters

3.

Guess. _____ centimeters

Check. _____ centimeters

4.

Guess. _____ centimeters

Check. _____ centimeters

Practice

Here are three practice problems for you.

Quick-Solve 1

Guess the perimeter of the shape.
Then check.

Guess. _____ centimeters

Check. _____ centimeters

Quick-Solve 2

Guess the perimeter of the shape.
Then check.

Guess. _____ centimeters

Check. _____ centimeters

Quick-Solve 3

Guess which shape has the greater perimeter.
Then check.

Guess. _____

Check. _____

Use What You Know

Now try guessing and checking to solve area problems.

Remember that *area* is the space inside a shape.

Look again at the four stickers. This time, try to guess the area of each one. Then check by using a centimeter ruler or centimeter cubes.

1.

Guess. _____ square centimeters

Check. _____ square centimeters

2.

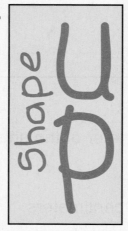

Guess. _____ square centimeters

Check. _____ square centimeters

3.

Guess. _____ square centimeters

Check. _____ square centimeters

4.

Guess. _____ square centimeters

Check. _____ square centimeters

Lesson 4 Solve It Your Way

Read each problem and decide how you will find the solution.

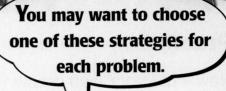

You may want to choose one of these strategies for each problem.

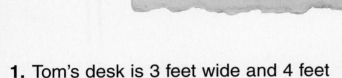

Draw a Picture
Guess and Check

1. Tom's desk is 3 feet wide and 4 feet long. What is the area of his desk?

2. Your class wants to cover the area around some trees with plastic. The area is 4 feet wide and 8 feet long. How much plastic do you need?

3. A window box is 8 inches long and 4 inches wide. What is its perimeter?

4. What is the perimeter of this shape?

5. What is the perimeter of this shape?

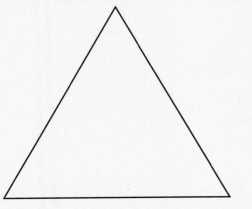

6. What is the area of this shape?

Practice

Now write your own problems using perimeter and area.

Quick-Solve 1

The answer to a problem is "24 square feet." Write your own problem to share with a friend. If your friend does not get an answer of 24 square feet, discuss how you might change the problem or the solution to match.

Quick-Solve 2

The answer to a problem is "12 inches." Write your own problem to share with a friend. If your friend does not get an answer of 12 inches, discuss how you might change the problem or the solution to match.

Quick-Solve 3

The answer to a problem is "16 centimeters." Write your own problem to share with a friend. If your friend does not get an answer of 16 centimeters, discuss how you might change the problem or the solution to match.

Applying Strategies

Review Show What You Know

Work in a small group.

Miss Morrow's class put together a mural showing the work they did during "Shape Up Our School" week. The students drew pictures to go on the mural. Each picture was a square or a rectangle. The finished mural had an area of 100 square feet. Use the dot paper to show the shapes that might have been on the mural.

. . . .
. . . .
. . . .
. . . .
. . . .
. . . .
. . . .
. . . .
. . . .
. . . .

1. How many rectangles did you use? _____

2. How many squares did you use? _____

3. How many pictures are on the mural? _____

Now you can choose from all these strategies!

Make a Model   **Draw a Picture**
Make an Estimate   **Guess and Check**

Read each problem and decide how you will find the solution.

1. Fifty-eight students put mulch in flower beds around the school. Thirty-two of them worked in the front area. How many worked in other areas?

2. Two buses take children to a balloon rally in Plano. One bus carries 44 children. The other carries 34 children. How many children in all are on these two buses?

3. The basket of one balloon has a length of 6 feet and a width of 4 feet. What is the perimeter of the basket?

4. The souvenir stand at the rally has 34 miniature balloons and 18 books about hot air balloons. How many more balloons than books are there?

5. Your teacher awards 32 ribbons for the "Shape Up Our School" project. She also gives out 45 stickers. How many more stickers than ribbons did she give away?

6. The perimeter of a square board is 36 feet. What does one of the sides measure?

Cumulative Review: Applying Strategies

7. There were 388 children who went to the "Shape Up Our School" awards program. There were 432 adults who went. How many people went to the program in all?

8. The target at one balloon rally was 8 feet wide and 9 feet long. What was the area of the target?

9. A balloon pilot flew 49 miles one weekend. She flew 32 miles the next weekend. How many miles did she fly in all?

10. At three balloon rallies, Dan won $147, $250, and $78 in prize money. About how much money did he receive for all these rallies?

11. Mrs. Gibbs is putting a border on her bulletin board. It is 6 feet long and 5 feet wide. How many feet of border will she need?

12. Guess the perimeter of this shape in centimeters. Then measure.

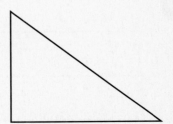

Guess _____   Measure _____

UNIT 3 Prehistoric Animals

Lesson 1   Write a Plan

Not all dinosaurs were tall giants. Some were short. Look at the list of five dinosaurs. Which one was tallest? Which one was shortest?

Heights of Five Dinosaurs

Stegosaurus	11 feet
Saltopus	8 inches
Triceratops	9 feet 6 inches
Hypsilophodon	24 inches
Dryosaurus	48 inches

Write a plan to solve the problem.

Step 1   Write in your own words what you need to find out.

_____

_____

Step 2   Write the facts that will be useful.

_____

_____

Step 3   Explain or show how you will solve the problem.

_____

_____

_____

_____

Writing a Plan: Comparisons and Data

Make a Graph

Try making a graph to solve the problem.

> **R**emember that
> 1 foot = 12 inches.

Look at the bar graph. Which dinosaur was shortest?

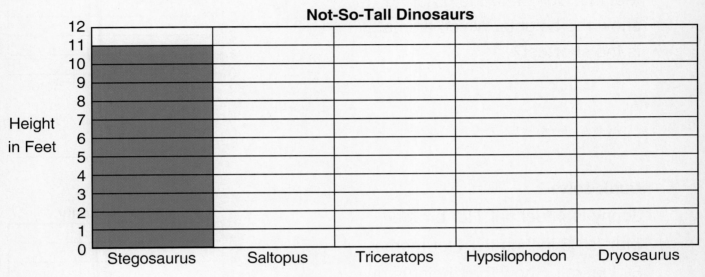

Not-So-Tall Dinosaurs

Height in Feet: 0–12

Stegosaurus   Saltopus   Triceratops   Hypsilophodon   Dryosaurus

1. Look at the bar graph. It is shaded to show the height of Stegosaurus, 11 feet. Look at the list to find the height of Saltopus. Then, shade the bar graph to show its height. Remember that 8 inches is less than 1 foot.

2. Complete the bar graph for the other dinosaurs. Remember to change inches to feet.

3. What is the tallest dinosaur shown on this graph? _____

4. What is the shortest dinosaur shown on this graph? _____

5. Are you taller than or shorter than a Triceratops? _____

Practice

Here are three practice problems for you.

Quick-Solve 1

Mike's cat is 12 inches tall. His dog is 2 feet tall. His horse is 5 feet tall. Complete the graph to show the heights. Which animal is the shortest?

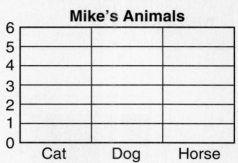

Mike's Animals

Height in Feet
6
5
4
3
2
1
0
Cat   Dog   Horse

Quick-Solve 2

Jenny is 4 feet tall. Her brother Max is 36 inches tall. Her mom is $5\frac{1}{2}$ feet tall. Show their heights on this graph. Who is tallest?

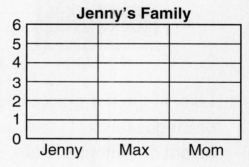

Jenny's Family

Height in Feet
6
5
4
3
2
1
0
Jenny   Max   Mom

Quick-Solve 3

The Troödon dinosaur was small but very smart. Troödon was $\frac{1}{2}$ foot taller than Hypsilophodon. How tall was Troödon?

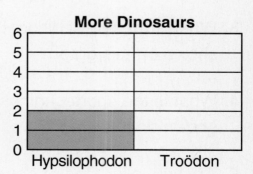

More Dinosaurs

Height in Feet
6
5
4
3
2
1
0
Hypsilophodon   Troödon

Applying Strategies

Use What You Know

Dinosaurs hatched from eggs.
How big were these eggs?

Use this bar graph to help answer the questions.

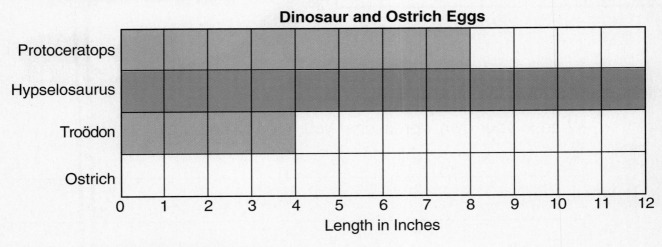

Dinosaur and Ostrich Eggs

Length in Inches

1. How long was a Troödon egg? _____ inches

2. How long was the egg of Hypselosaurus? _____ inches

3. How long was the egg of Protoceratops? _____ inches

4. The largest bird alive today is the ostrich. Its egg is
   6 inches long. Show this on the bar graph.

5. Compare the ostrich egg to any other egg on the
   graph. What do you notice?

_____

_____

_____

_____

Lesson 2 Write a Plan

Suppose you have 10 toy dinosaurs like the ones shown. Sort them by color. Which color appears the most? Which colors appear the least?

Write a plan to solve the problem.

Step 1

Write in your own words what you need to find out.

_____

_____

Step 2

Write the facts that will be useful.

_____

_____

Step 3

Explain or show how you will solve the problem.

_____

_____

_____

_____

_____

Writing a Plan: Comparisons and Data

Make a Graph

Try making a graph to solve the problem.

Look at the toy dinosaurs. Make a bar graph to show the colors you have. For this graph, draw your own bars first. Then shade them in.

1. Complete the graph. The first two bars have been drawn and shaded for you. Use different colors to shade the remaining bars.

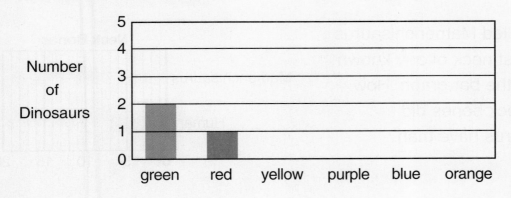

2. Look at your graph. Which color appears the most? _____

3. Which colors appear the least? _____

4. Which colors appear twice? _____ , _____
Explain how the graph helps you find out.

_____

_____

_____

Practice

Here are three practice problems for you.

Quick-Solve 1

Sandy has 10 dinosaur figures. She has 6 meat eaters and 4 plant eaters. Make a bar graph showing Sandy's collection.

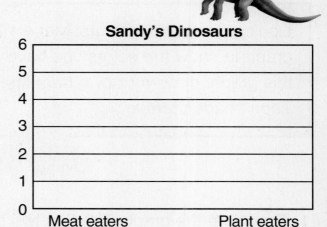

Quick-Solve 2

A dinosaur called Mamenchisaurus had the longest neck of any known animal. Read the bar graph. How many more neck bones did Mamenchisaurus have than a human?

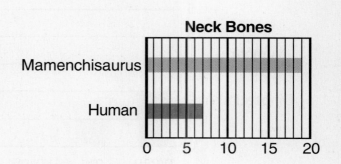

Quick-Solve 3

Shozo has 20 dinosaurs. He has 15 plant eaters and 5 meat eaters. Finish this bar graph.

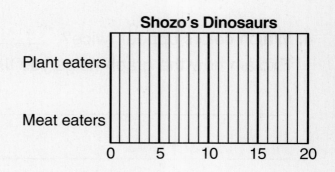

Use What You Know

Some of the toy animals are not really dinosaurs. Look at these 10 prehistoric animals. Make a graph showing dinosaurs and animals that are not dinosaurs.

Dinosaurs   **Not Dinosaurs**

1. Make a bar graph to show the numbers of prehistoric animals.

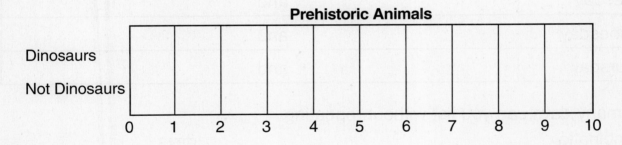

Prehistoric Animals

Dinosaurs

Not Dinosaurs

0   1   2   3   4   5   6   7   8   9   10

2. How many are dinosaurs? _____

3. How many are not dinosaurs? _____

4. Now get your own group of 10 prehistoric animal figures. Make a bar graph to show the number of dinosaurs and the number that are not dinosaurs.

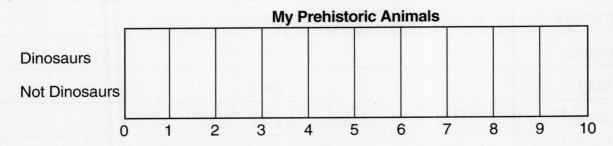

My Prehistoric Animals

Dinosaurs

Not Dinosaurs

0   1   2   3   4   5   6   7   8   9   10

Lesson 3   Make an Organized List

You have made a graph to solve problems.
Now try making an organized list.

> You have 3 colors of toy Brachiosaurus. Your toy cave holds only 2 of them at a time. Each day you place 2 different animals in the cave. How many days until you repeat a combination? (A yellow and blue combination is the same as a blue and yellow combination.)

1. Make a list to show the color combinations.

Day	Animals in the Cave
Monday	and
Tuesday	and
Wednesday	and
Thursday	and

2. How many days can you list without repeating
   a combination?   _____ days

3. Suppose you add a fourth color.
   How many days can you list now?   _____ days

Day	Animals in the Cave
Monday	and
Tuesday	and
Wednesday	and
Thursday	and
Friday	and
Saturday	and

Practice

Here are three practice problems for you.

Quick-Solve 1

You have 1 red toy animal. You put a yellow, green, orange, and blue animal in a bag. Without looking you pick 1 animal. List all the possible combinations you can make with 1 red animal and 1 animal of another color.

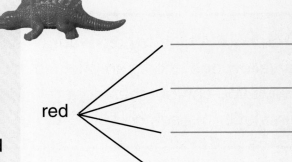

red ⟨ _____
_____
_____
_____

Quick-Solve 2

You have some toy prehistoric animals. Some are meat eaters. Some are plant eaters. Some are red. Some are blue. You want to show a plant eater and a meat eater of each color. List the type and color of animals you will need.

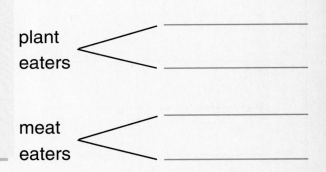

plant eaters ⟨ _____
_____

meat eaters ⟨ _____
_____

Quick-Solve 3

Mandy has 4 toy dinosaurs. Each is a different color: red, yellow, green, and blue. She wants to put them in a row. She wants the yellow and green dinosaurs on the ends. List the different ways she can arrange them. Use only the first letter of each color.

__y__, _____, _____, __g__

_____, _____, _____, _____

_____, _____, _____, _____

_____, _____, _____, _____

Use What You Know

Now try making an organized list to
solve another combination problem.

You have a blue toy dinosaur. Then you get
a yellow one and a red one. List all the different
ways you can put them in a row. Use only the
first letter of each color.

1. Make a list to show the
   combinations of blue, yellow,
   and red dinosaurs.

   _____, _____, _____

   _____, _____, _____

   _____, _____, _____

   _____, _____, _____

   _____, _____, _____

   _____, _____, _____

2. Try this again with blue, orange,
   and green dinosaurs.

   _____, _____, _____

   _____, _____, _____

   _____, _____, _____

   _____, _____, _____

   _____, _____, _____

   _____, _____, _____

3. Compare your lists. Write about how the lists are
   alike and different.

   _____

   _____

   _____

Making an Organized List: Comparisons and Data

Lesson 4 Solve It Your Way

Read each problem and decide how you will find the solution.

You may want to choose one of these strategies for each problem.

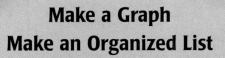

Make a Graph
Make an Organized List

Solve.

1. Danny has some animal figures. He has 5 plant eaters and 2 meat eaters. Complete the graph showing his collection.

Danny's Animals

Plant eaters

Meat eaters

0 1 2 3 4 5 6

2. If Danny got 3 more meat eaters, how would you change the graph?

Danny's Animals

Plant eaters

Meat eaters

0 1 2 3 4 5 6

3. You have 3 toy Dimetrodons. They are red, green, and purple. List all the ways you can put them in a row with purple in the middle.

4. Suppose 4 Brachiosaurus dinosaurs (named A, B, C, and D) see a treetop to munch. They are too big for all to munch at the same time. Only 3 can fit. List all the combinations of dinosaurs that can take turns.

Practice

Now write your own problems using data, graphs, and combinations.

Quick-Solve 1

The answer to a problem is this graph.
What might the question be?

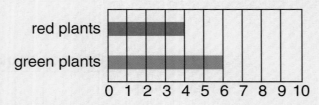

red plants
green plants

0 1 2 3 4 5 6 7 8 9 10

Quick-Solve 2

The answer to a problem is this list.
What might the question be?

blue and green
blue and purple
green and purple

Quick-Solve 3

The answer to a problem is this list.
What might the question be?

D, E, F
D, F, E
E, F, D
E, D, F
F, D, E
F, E, D

Review   Show What You Know

Work with a partner.
Use red and blue animal figures.

1. Place 12 animal figures in a bag.
Use some red and some blue.

2. Without looking, take out 1 animal. Is it red or blue?
Make a tally mark to record your answer. Put the
animal back in the bag. Repeat this 18 times.

Red	
Blue	

3. Use your tally table to make a bar graph.

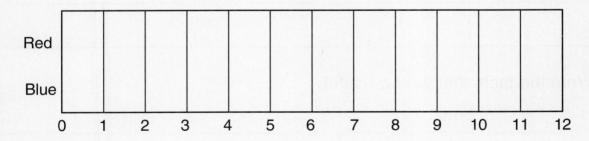

4. How many red animals are in the bag? How many
blue? Do these match your graph? Why do you think
that happened?

_____

_____

_____

_____

UNIT 4 Super Sports!

Lesson 1 Write a Plan

The table on the right shows several popular sports and the number of players on each team. Each of these sports is played by 2 teams at a time. How many players are there in all for each game?

Sports Teams

Sport	Players on Each Team
Baseball	9
Soccer	11
Basketball	5
Volleyball	6
Badminton	2
Lacrosse	10

Write a plan to solve the problem.

Step 1

Write in your own words what you need to find out.

_____

_____

Step 2

Write the facts that will be useful.

_____

_____

Step 3

Explain or show how you will solve the problem.

_____

_____

_____

Writing a Plan: Multiplication and Division

Make a Table

Try making a table to solve the problem.

Using objects may help you find the products.

Multiply to complete the table. Look at the number of players on each team. Multiply by the number of teams in each game. How many players in all are in each game?

Sports Games

Sport	Players on Each Team	Players in the Game
Baseball	9	
Soccer	11	
Basketball	5	
Volleyball	6	
Badminton	2	
Lacrosse	10	

1. Each sport in the table is played by 2 teams. Multiply by 2 to find each missing number. Fill in the correct numbers in the table.

2. Compare the number of players in each game. How can you list the sports in the table to make comparing them easier?

_____

_____

3. Which sport has the greatest number of players in a game? _____

4. Which sport has the fewest number of players on a team? _____

5. If there are 8 teams in a soccer tournament, how many players would compete? _____ players

Practice

Here are three problems for you.

Quick-Solve 1

Mira and Sue competed in a track meet. Mira ran 5 races and Sue ran 3. Each ran 3 laps per race. How many laps in all did they run in the track meet?

	Number of Races	Total Number of Laps
Mira	5	
Sue	3	

Quick-Solve 2

The Panthers basketball team made three times as many baskets as free throws in each quarter of their last game. How many baskets did they make in the third and fourth quarters?

	Quarter 1	Quarter 2	Quarter 3	Quarter 4
Free Throws	4	3	6	5
Baskets	12	9		

Quick-Solve 3

The Bulldogs football team scored twice as many field goals as touchdowns. How many touchdowns did they score in each game? If a field goal is worth 3 points and a touchdown is worth 6 points, how many points did they score in Game 2?

	Game 1	Game 2	Game 3
Field Goals	2	6	4
Touchdowns			

Applying Strategies

Use What You Know

Multiply or divide to complete the table. How many players are on each team? How many shoes are worn in the game?

Sports Shoes

Sport	Players on Each Team	Shoes in the Game
Softball	9	36
Football		44
Tennis (Singles)		4
Ice Hockey	6	
Kickball	9	

1. Some students thought it might be fun to find the number of shoes on their favorite sports teams. How will you find the missing numbers?

_____

_____

2. Remember that 2 teams play in a game and each player wears 2 shoes. Find "softball" in the table. What number would you use to multiply the players on each team to find the number of shoes in the game? $9 \times$ _____ $= 36$

3. Multiply or divide to complete the table.

4. Did you multiply or divide to find the number of players on a football team? Why?

_____

_____

5. Did you multiply or divide to find the number of shoes in an ice hockey game? Why?

_____

_____

Lesson 2   Write a Plan

Coach Rodgers is selling season tickets for the school's sports events. To help her remember the ticket prices for each sport, she made a table. How many games are played in a season for each sport?

Sports Tickets

Sport	Season Ticket Price	Price per Ticket
Softball	$64	$8
Football	$72	$12
Basketball	$90	$10
Tennis	$35	$5
Soccer	$88	$11

Write a plan to solve the problem.

Step 1   Write in your own words what you need to find out.

_____

_____

Step 2   Write the facts that will be useful.

_____

_____

Step 3   Explain or show how you will solve the problem.

_____

_____

_____

_____

_____

Make a Table

Try making a table to solve the problem.

> **D**ivide to complete the table. Look at the price of season tickets. Divide by the price per ticket. How many games are played in a season?

Using objects may help you find the quotients.

Ticket Prices

Sport	Season Ticket Price	Price per Ticket	Number of Games in a Season
Softball	$64	$8	
Football	$72	$12	
Basketball	$90	$10	
Tennis	$35	$5	
Soccer	$88	$11	

1. Divide the season ticket price by the price per ticket. Fill in the correct numbers in the table.

2. Which sport has the greatest number of games per season? _____

3. Which sport has the fewest number of games per season? _____

4. Football tickets for each game are $12 per adult and $6 per child under twelve years of age. If Tommy's father bought season tickets for football for one adult and one child, how much did he pay?

Practice

Here are three problems for you.

Quick-Solve 1

Coach Marks has to buy items for his tennis team. There are 8 players on his team. How much will it cost to buy each item for the whole team?

	Cost per Item	Cost per Team
Tennis Balls	$4	
Rackets	$55	
Visors	$9	

Quick-Solve 2

Albert is raising money for his school by selling tickets to his team's soccer games. Each ticket costs $3. How much money does he raise for each game if he sells the number of tickets shown in the table?

	Number of Tickets Sold	Amount of Money Raised
Game 1	21	
Game 2	17	
Game 3	12	
Game 4	32	

Quick-Solve 3

Mrs. Wahl must buy jerseys for the school's kickball and softball teams. The jerseys cost $9 each. She has $200 to spend. Does she have enough money?

	Number of Players on the Team	Total Price of the Jerseys
Kickball	9	
Softball	10	

Applying Strategies

Use What You Know

Use the table. Multiply or divide to fill in the missing ticket prices. What is the special lower price for tickets? What is the special lower price for season tickets?

Special Ticket Prices

Sport	Season Ticket Price	Number of Games in a Season	Price per Ticket
Softball	$48	8	$6
Football	$60	6	
Basketball		9	$8
Tennis	$28	7	
Soccer	$40	8	

1. Family members of the players get special lower prices for season tickets. Coach Rodgers made a table to show the prices. How will you find the missing ticket prices in the table?

_____

2. Remember that each sport has a different number of games in a season. Find "softball" in the table. What operation was used to find the price per ticket? What operation was used to find the season ticket price?

_____

3. Multiply or divide to complete the table.

4. Did you multiply or divide to find the season ticket price for basketball? Why? _____

_____

5. Did you multiply or divide to find the price per ticket for soccer? Why? _____

_____

Lesson 3   Find a Pattern

You have used tables to solve problems.
Now try finding a pattern to solve a problem.

Look at the drawing of a swimming pool. The pool is divided into 8 lanes. The lanes are a certain number of yards wide. Find the pattern to fill in the missing yard numbers.

Swimming Lanes

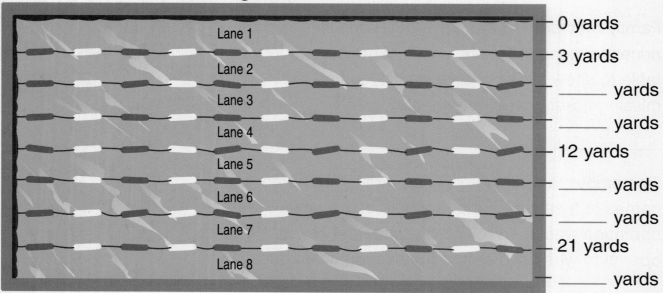

Lane 1 — 0 yards
— 3 yards
Lane 2
— _____ yards
Lane 3
— _____ yards
Lane 4
— 12 yards
Lane 5
— _____ yards
Lane 6
— _____ yards
Lane 7
— 21 yards
Lane 8
— _____ yards

1. Fill in the missing yard numbers.

2. What pattern can you find in the number of yards?

_____

3. How many yards is the total width of the swimming pool?   _____ yards

4. Suppose a larger pool has 10 lanes. If each lane is the same width as in the smaller pool, how wide is the larger pool? How do you know?

_____

Finding a Pattern: Mixed Operations

Practice

Here are three practice problems for you.

Quick-Solve 1

In the first game of a tournament, Joey scores 10 points. In the second game he scores 15 points, and in the third he scores 20 points. If the pattern continues, how many points will he score in the fourth game of the tournament?

Quick-Solve 2

Kofi trains for a bicycle race. He rides 3 miles on Monday, 5 miles on Tuesday, and 7 miles on Wednesday. If he continues this pattern, how far will he ride on Thursday and Friday?

Quick-Solve 3

At the beginning of the baseball season, Coach Lee discovers that one of the jerseys is missing. The jerseys are numbered in a pattern. Help Coach Lee find the missing jersey number.

42 49 ? 63 70

Use What You Know

Look at the drawing of a football field. Some of the yard lines are marked on the drawing. Find the pattern to fill in the missing yard lines.

Football Field

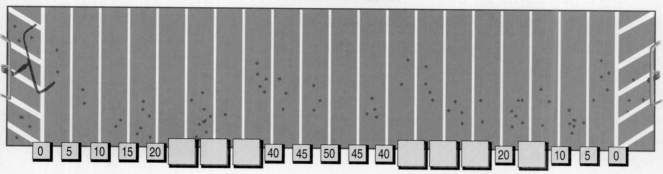

| 0 | 5 | 10 | 15 | 20 | | | | 40 | 45 | 50 | 45 | 40 | | | | 20 | | 10 | 5 | 0 |

1. What patterns can you find in the yard lines on the football field?

_____

_____

2. Fill in the missing yard lines.

3. How many yards is the total length of the football field? _____ yards

4. A kicker punted the ball on the 50 yard line. The ball dropped 35 yards away. On which yard line did the ball land? How do you know?

_____

_____

Finding a Pattern: Mixed Operations

Lesson 4   Solve It Your Way

Read each problem and decide how you will find the solution.

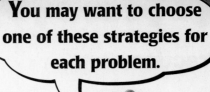

You may want to choose one of these strategies for each problem.

Make a Table
Find a Pattern

1. In the first game of the season, Jill scores 8 points. In the second game, she scores 12, and in the third she scores 16. If her streak continues, how many points will she score in the fourth game?

2. Carla found 3 golf balls in 5 minutes. She found 6 balls in 10 minutes. If she continues at the same pace, how long will it take her to find 12 golf balls?

3. The Marvin Mavericks won 8 games and lost 12 their first season. The second season they won 10 and lost 10. If this pattern continues, how many games will they win their third season? How many games will they lose?

4. In each game, Maria's team scores double the points of the game before. In each game, Julie's team scores 5 more points than the game before. Who played on each team? How do you know? Whose team won the last game?

	Games Won	Games Lost
Season 1	8	12
Season 2	10	10
Season 3		

Teams	Game 1	Game 2	Game 3	Game 4
Sharks	25	30	35	
Tigers	6	12	24	

Application: Choosing a Strategy

Practice

Now write your own problems using multiplication and division facts.

Quick-Solve 1

The missing number in a pattern is 18. Write your own number pattern and share it with a friend. If your friend does not find the missing number, discuss how you might change the problem or the solution to match.

Quick-Solve 2

The missing number in a table is $6. Write your own problem to share with a friend. If your friend does not get the same answer, discuss how you might change the problem or solution to match.

Quick-Solve 3

The missing number in a pattern is 25. Write your own number pattern and share it with a friend. If your friend does not find the missing number, discuss how you might change the problem or the solution to match.

 Applying Strategies

Review Show What You Know

Work in a small group.
You have been asked to design a banner for your school sports stars.

1. There are 16 all-star players that you can represent with a star.

2. Show one way you could arrange the stars.

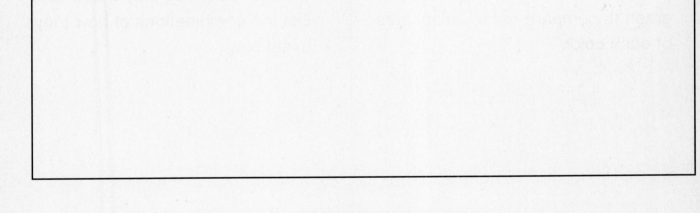

3. Now show two other ways you could arrange 16 stars.

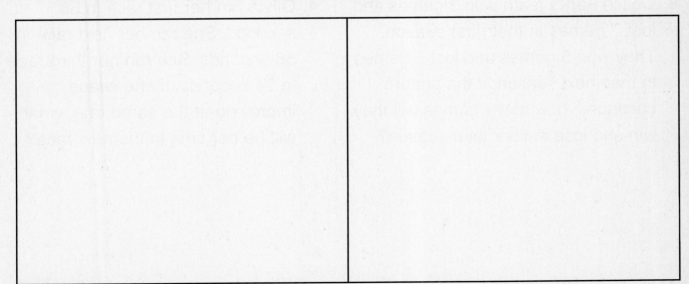

Now you can choose from all these strategies.

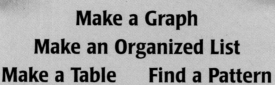

Make a Graph
Make an Organized List
Make a Table   Find a Pattern

Read each problem and decide how you will find the solution.

1. Amy has 3 blue toy dinosaurs. She has 4 yellow toy dinosaurs. Make a graph to compare her toy dinosaurs of each color.

2. Ted, Mike, and Alana play tennis after school. They play 2 at a time. List the combinations of how they might play.

3. Coach Park's team won 3 games and lost 7 games in their first season. They won 5 games and lost 5 games in their next season. If the pattern continues, how many games will they win and lose in their third season?

4. Olivia ran her first race in 58 seconds. She ran her next race in 56 seconds. She ran her third race in 54 seconds. If she keeps improving at the same rate, what will be her time in the next race?

5. Linda and her friends have toy dinosaurs. Linda has 4 green ones. Tim has 2 red ones. Janet has 5 purple ones. Make a graph to compare the number of dinosaurs.

6. Sean has 3 toy dinosaurs. They are blue, yellow, and orange. List the different ways he can arrange them in a row.

7. Lisa is making a table of ticket prices for the basketball games. There are 7 home games this season. A season ticket for the best seats costs $35. A season ticket for discount seats costs $28. Make a table to show these amounts and the price per game for the tickets.

8. Coach Levi told the swim team to swim 9 laps, then 7 laps, then 5 laps. If the pattern continues, how many laps will they swim next? What would the number of laps be after that?

UNIT 5 What's Cooking?

Lesson 1   Write a Plan

> Your school is having a pizza party. The principal orders 100 pizzas. 22 pizzas have olives. How many pizzas do not have olives?

Write a plan to solve the problem.

Step 1 Write in your own words what you need to find out.

_____

_____

Step 2 Write the facts that will be useful.

_____

_____

Step 3 Explain or show how you will solve the problem.

_____

_____

_____

_____

_____

Choose the Operation

Try choosing an operation to solve the problem.

Choose whether to add or subtract to find how many pizzas do not have olives. Add and subtract the numbers in the problem. Look at both solutions. Read the problem again. Decide which solution is reasonable. If 22 out of 100 pizzas have olives, how many pizzas do not have olives?

Choose between addition and subtraction to solve the problem.

1. If you add, what answer do you get?

   100
   +22

2. If you subtract, what answer do you get?

   100
   −22

3. Read the problem again. Which solution is reasonable? How do you know?

_____

_____

4. How many pizzas do not have olives? _____ pizzas

5. Fifty-nine of the pizzas without olives were eaten at the party. How many pizzas without olives were left over? How do you know?

_____

_____

Practice

Here are three practice problems for you.

Quick-Solve 1

Three teachers were asked to bring paper plates for the school's pizza party. Mrs. Dain brought a package of 75 plates. Mr. Benton brought 2 packages of 50 plates each. Ms. Read had 43 plates left over from a previous party. How many more paper plates are needed for a total of 300 plates?

Quick-Solve 2

Tanya and Rosa want to make cookies for the party. Tanya's recipe makes 3 dozen cookies. Rosa's recipe makes 48 cookies. Whose recipe makes more cookies? How many more?

Quick-Solve 3

Roberto wants to make fruit punch for the party. The recipe calls for 128 ounces of ginger ale. He already has three 32-ounce bottles. Will he need to buy more ginger ale? How do you know?

Use What You Know

When the school party began, there were 300 brownies, 1 for each person. When the party was over, there were 29 brownies left. If each person ate only 1 brownie, how many people ate brownies at the party?

Choose between addition and subtraction to solve the problem.

1. If you add, what answer do you get?

    300
    +29
    ———

2. If you subtract, what answer do you get?

    300
    −29
    ———

3. Read the problem again. Which solution is reasonable? How do you know?

_____

_____

4. How many people ate brownies? _____ people

5. The next day, students in the third grade class ate the remaining brownies for an afternoon snack. Four brownies were not eaten. If each student had only 1 brownie, how many students were in the class? How do you know?

_____

_____

Lesson 2   Write a Plan

At the pizza party, there were 27 pizzas with mushrooms. For each of those, 3 mushrooms were cut up and used. How many mushrooms were used for the pizza party?

Write a plan to solve the problem.

Step 1   Write in your own words what you need to find out.

_____

_____

Step 2   Write the facts that will be useful.

_____

_____

Step 3   Explain or show how you will solve the problem.

_____

_____

_____

_____

_____

_____

Choose the Operation

Try choosing an operation to solve the problem.

Multiply to combine equal groups. Divide to separate equal groups.

> Choose whether to multiply or divide to find how many mushrooms were used for the pizza party. Multiply and divide the numbers in the problem. Look at both solutions. Read the problem again. Decide which solution is reasonable. If 3 mushrooms were used for 1 pizza, how many mushrooms were used for all 27 pizzas?

1. If you multiply, what answer do you get?

$$\begin{array}{r} 27 \\ \times 3 \\ \hline \end{array}$$

2. If you divide, what answer do you get?

$3\overline{)27}$

3. Read the problem again. Which solution is reasonable? How do you know?

_____

_____

_____

4. How many mushrooms were used for the pizza party?

_____ mushrooms

5. One chopped onion will cover 4 pizzas. How many onions are needed to make 32 onion pizzas?

_____ onions

Practice

Here are three practice problems for you.

Quick-Solve 1

Maria's pizza sauce recipe makes 4 cups of sauce. If she needs only 1 cup of sauce for each pizza, how many batches of the recipe does she need to make 12 pizzas?

Quick-Solve 2

Brian likes lots of cheese on his pizza. He tops each pizza with $\frac{1}{2}$ cup of mozzarella and $\frac{1}{4}$ cup of parmesan. He wants to make 5 pizzas. How much of each kind of cheese will Brian use?

Quick-Solve 3

If each pizza is cut into 6 slices and each person eats 2 slices, how many people will 27 pizzas feed?

Use What You Know

Choose between multiplication and division to solve the problem.

Look at the recipe. The class plans to make chalupas. If the students grate 8 cups of cheese, how many chalupas can they make?

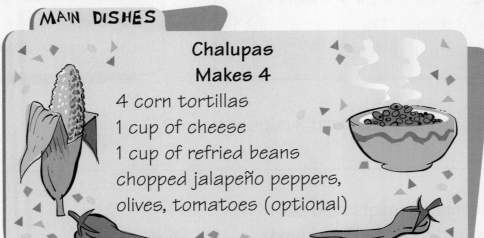

MAIN DISHES

Chalupas
Makes 4

4 corn tortillas
1 cup of cheese
1 cup of refried beans
chopped jalapeño peppers,
olives, tomatoes (optional)

1. If you multiply, what answer do you get?

$$\begin{array}{r} 8 \\ \times 4 \\ \hline \end{array}$$

2. If you divide, what answer do you get?

$$4\overline{)8}$$

3. Read the problem again. Which solution is reasonable? How do you know?

_____

_____

4. How many chalupas can they make? _____ chalupas

5. Suppose the students cut each chalupa into 2 parts.

How many pieces will they make? _____ pieces

Lesson 3 Use Logical Reasoning

You have chosen operations to solve problems. Now try using logical reasoning to solve.

Side Dishes

Jamaican Rice
and Beans
Serves 8

1 cup of beans
4 cups of coconut milk
3 cups of water
3 cups of rice
2 green onions
salt, pepper, and garlic

Cheryl's recipe serves 8 people. She wants to make her recipe for the 24 students in her class. Cheryl thinks: "Do I need 3 cups of beans or 30 cups of beans?"

1. What kind of container might hold 3 cups of beans?

_____

2. What kind of container might hold 30 cups of beans and all of the other food? _____

3. Which is more reasonable: 3 cups of beans or 30 cups of beans? How do you know?

_____

_____

4. What can Cheryl do to the recipe to find what amounts are needed? Explain how you can figure it out.

_____

_____

5. Will Cheryl need 12 cups of coconut milk or 8 cups? How do you know?

_____

_____

Using Logical Reasoning: Mixed Operations

Practice

Here are three practice problems for you.

Quick-Solve 1

The third grade has 4 classes. The largest class has 30 students. The smallest class has 20 students. How many students might be in the third grade? Which is a more logical answer, 1,000 or 100 students? How do you know?

Quick-Solve 2

A Spanish rice recipe serves 8 people. It uses 3 cups of rice. You want to double the recipe. How much rice will you need? Which is a more logical answer, 16 cups or 6 cups? How do you know?

Quick-Solve 3

Jasmine wants to share her Hawaiian monkey bread. Each loaf is enough for 4 students. How many loaves will she need for 25 students? Which is a more logical answer, 100 loaves or 7 loaves? How do you know?

Use What You Know

Now try using logical reasoning to answer another problem.

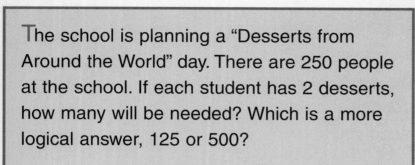

The school is planning a "Desserts from Around the World" day. There are 250 people at the school. If each student has 2 desserts, how many will be needed? Which is a more logical answer, 125 or 500?

1. Imagine a group of 3 students. Each student has 2 desserts. Make a drawing of each person with 2 desserts. Does your picture show more than or less than 3 desserts?

2. Imagine a class with 25 students. Each student will have 2 desserts. Will there be more than 25 or less than 25 desserts? How do you know?

_____

_____

3. What is a reasonable answer for 250 students with 2 desserts each? How do you know?

_____

_____

Using Logical Reasoning: Mixed Operations

Lesson 4   Solve It Your Way

Read each problem and decide how you will find the solution.

You may want to choose one of these strategies for each problem.

Choose the Operation
Use Logical Reasoning

1. A recipe makes 30 meatballs. There are 3 meatballs in each serving. How many servings can you make?

2. Sarah has 5 chocolate bars. She splits each bar into 4 pieces. How many pieces does she have?

3. A recipe makes 4 servings of Trinidad Peanut Punch. One recipe uses 3 cups of milk. You have 6 cups of milk. How many servings can you make?

4. A matzo cake uses 6 pieces of matzo (flat bread). Ben wants to make 3 cakes. How many pieces of matzo does he need?

5. You plan a party for 18 teachers. You will serve muffins. You expect each teacher to take 0, 1, or 2 muffins. About how many muffins do you need? Which is a more logical answer, fewer than 40 or about 100 muffins? Explain.

6. Your dad bought a package of 60 oatmeal cookies. You can have 3 cookies a day as an after-school snack. Will the package last 20 days or 180 days? Explain.

Practice

Now write your own problems using multiplication, division, and logical reasoning.

Quick-Solve 1

The answer to a problem is 4. What might the question be? Write your own problem to share with a friend. If your friend does not get an answer of 4, discuss how you might change the problem or the solution to match.

Quick-Solve 2

The answer to a problem is 10. What might the question be? Write your own problem to share with a friend. If your friend does not get an answer of 10, discuss how you might change the problem or the solution to match.

Quick-Solve 3

The answer to a problem is 80. What might the question be? Write your own problem to share with a friend. If your friend does not get an answer of 80, discuss how you might change the problem or the solution to match.

Applying Strategies

Review   Show What You Know

Work with a partner. Show all your work.

Ants-on-a-Log
Serves 2
1 stalk celery
1 tablespoon peanut butter
10 raisins

Plan to make "Ants-on-a-Log" for the students in your class. How many raisins will you need? How much celery will you need?

1. Count the students in your class. Each student will get 2 servings. How many servings do you need to make?

    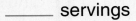 servings

2. If each serving has 5 raisins, how many raisins will you need for your class?   _____ raisins

3. How many stalks of celery will you need?   _____ stalks

4. Suppose each student in your class invites 1 friend to your class party. Each person will get 2 servings. How will you change your party plans?

_____

_____

_____

_____

_____

Final Review

Now you can choose from all these strategies!

Read each problem and decide how you will find the solution.

Make a Model	Make an Estimate
Draw a Picture	Guess and Check
Make a Graph	Make an Organized List
Make a Table	Choose the Operation
Find a Pattern	Use Logical Reasoning

1. Sixty students brought food for a bake sale at the fair. Thirty-one of them brought cookies. How many did not bring cookies?

2. On a school field trip, one bus broke down. The 36 students on the bus had to move to the other 3 buses. If they moved in equal groups, how many students were added to each bus?

3. Mr. Jackson planted 36 flower seeds and 45 vegetable seeds in his garden. About how many seeds in all did he plant?

4. The souvenir stand at a balloon rally had mugs for $8, visors for $10, and caps for $12. If you had $20 to spend, what could you buy at the rally?

Cumulative Review: Applying Strategies

5. Guess the perimeter of this shape in centimeters. Then measure.

_____ centimeters

6. Guess the area in square centimeters of this shape. Then check.

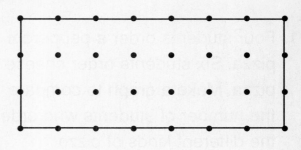

_____ square centimeters

7. The perimeter of a square board is 40 inches. What is the length of each side?

8. The target at a balloon rally was 6 feet wide and 8 feet long. What was the area of the target?

9. Miss Lewis made cupcakes for her class of 27 students. She put 3 jelly beans on each cupcake. Did she use 9 or 81 jelly beans in all? Which answer makes the most sense? How do you know?

10. Mr. Perez's cake recipe uses 3 cups of flour. He made 3 cakes. Did he use 9 cups or 1 cup of flour? Which answer makes the most sense? How do you know?

11. Four students order a pepperoni pizza. Six students order cheese pizza. Make a graph to compare the number of students who order the different kinds of pizza.

12. Ivan is putting a baseball card, a football card, and a soccer card in his scrapbook. Make a list to show the different ways he can line these up in a row.

13. Mrs. Chan buys shirts for the little league teams. Ten shirts cost a total of $100. Twenty shirts cost a total of $180. Thirty shirts cost $240 in all. Use a table to list these prices. Then find the price per shirt for each group. Which is the best bargain?

14. Suppose you were delivering mail to the mailboxes below. Some of the numbers are missing. Look for patterns in the numbers. Then fill in the missing mailbox numbers.